MORE WATER, PLEASE!

ANIMALS IN DRY PLACES

Jack Lantz

Contents

Rigby

A Harcourt Achieve Imprint

www.Rigby.com
1-800-531-5015

Animals and Water

All living things need water, and animals are no different. For some animals, getting water is easy. But for other animals, it is not easy at all! These animals have found amazing ways to get water even in very dry **habitats.**

Run, Wildebeests, Run!

Wildebeests are large animals that live in the dry African grasslands and woodlands. They live in large groups and travel more than 300 miles each year following the rains in search of water. The wildebeests begin migrating in November, following the rains south toward better grasslands.

The herds stop from January to March to give birth to their calves. After the calves are born, the herds gather and move west, following the rains again. They look for fresh grass and water between April and June.

The journey can be full of danger. Lions, cheetahs, and hyenas hunt for wildebeests in the open grasslands. From July to October, the wildebeests return north and east, back toward the waters they left in November. Many wildebeests die crossing rivers where hungry crocodiles wait.

Often more than one million wildebeests make this journey together. It's the largest **migration** on Earth!

Wildebeest Migration

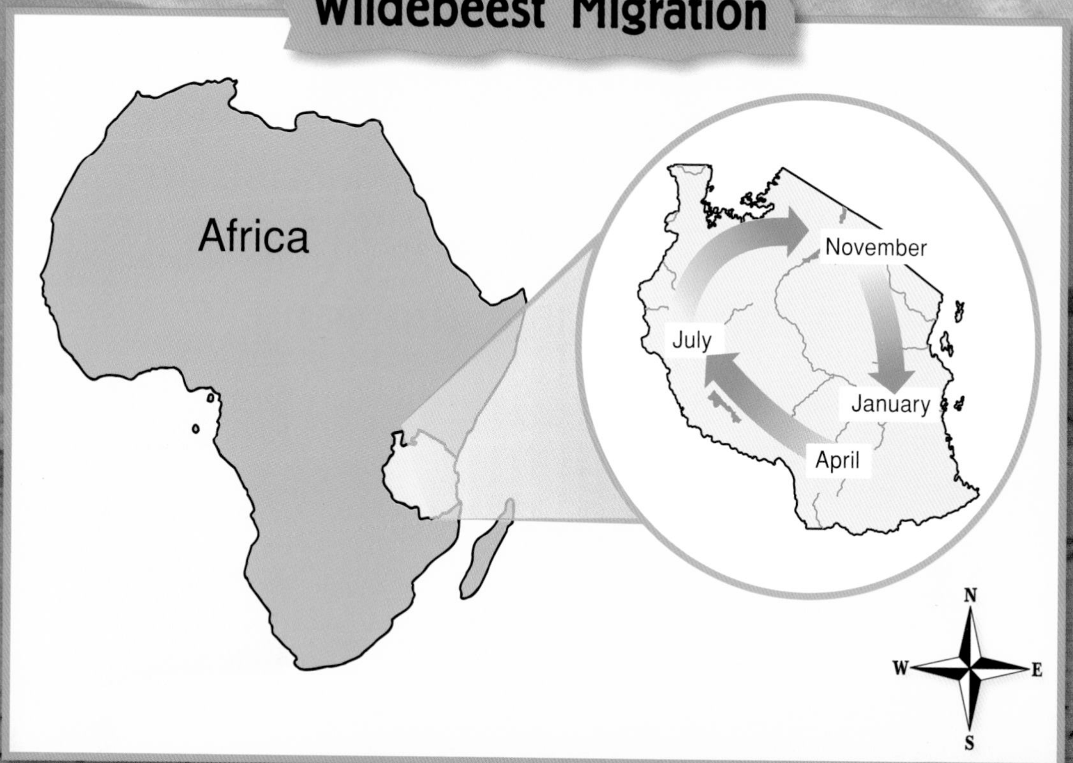

Africa

November

July

January

April

N
W E
S

Walk, Fish, Walk!

A snakehead fish is a fish whose head looks like a snake. With large mouths and big teeth, these fish grow more than three feet long. But that's not what makes them amazing.

Most fish get oxygen from water through their gills. But because the snakehead fish live in shallow ponds, these fish take in oxygen from the air. If a pond dries up, the snakehead will bury itself in the mud to stay moist until the rains come. Snakehead fish can even walk across land to find another pond or puddle. Snakeheads can walk on wet land for three days at a time!

a snakehead fish out of water

Water for All

Each of these amazing animals finds a different way to adapt to its environment so it has enough water to live. As environments change, amazing animals continue to find new ways to live.

Glossary

cocoons coverings that protect certain animals

habitats places where plants or animals live in nature

hibernate to sleep or rest for a long time

migration the act of large groups of animals moving during certain seasons from one place to another

Dig, Frogs, Dig!

Did you know that frogs soak in water and breathe through their skin? If their skin dries out, they will die. So how do frogs live in a dry desert?

Before the dry season comes, desert frogs dig into the ground and **hibernate**. If the ground dries out, they make **cocoons** around their skin that stay wet inside as the frogs breathe. This protects the frog from the desert heat. When the rains come, the frogs dig themselves out, eat everything they can, and then lay thousands of eggs in puddles of water.

One day later, tadpoles hatch from the eggs. Tadpoles now have about four weeks to grow into frogs. They grow fast because the puddles don't last long, and without water to swim in, the tadpoles will die.

As the desert dries up, the frogs bury themselves again and wait for the next year's rains.

tadpoles